Rite Passage

Birthdays

Paul Mason

www.heinemann.co.uk/library
Visit our website to find out more information about **Heinemann Library** books.

To order:
☎ Phone 44 (0) 1865 888066
📄 Send a fax to 44 (0) 1865 314091
💻 Visit the Heinemann Bookshop at www.heinemann.co.uk/library to browse our catalogue and order online.

First published in Great Britain by Heinemann Library, Halley Court, Jordan Hill, Oxford OX2 8EJ, part of Harcourt Education.
Heinemann is a registered trademark of Harcourt Education Ltd.

Editorial: Jilly Attwood and Claire Throp
Design: David Poole and Geoff Ward
Picture Research: Rosie Garai and Su Alexander
Production: Séverine Ribierre

Originated by Ambassador Litho Ltd
Printed in China by W K T

ISBN 978 0 431 17715 1 (hardback)
ISBN 0 431 17715 5 (hardback)
07 06 05 04 03
10 9 8 7 6 5 4 3 2 1

ISBN 978 0 431 17722 9 (paperback)
ISBN 0 431 17722 8 (paperback)
08
10 9 8 7 6 5 4 3

British Library Cataloguing in Publication Data
Mason, Paul
Birthdays - (Rites of Passage)
392.1'2
A full catalogue record for this book is available from the British Library.

Acknowledgements
The publishers would like to thank the following for permission to reproduce photographs: Alamy Images pp. **24**, **27**; Ann & Bury Peerless p. **25**; Christine Osborne p. **26**; Corbis pp. **6** (Barbara Peacock), **8** (Dianna Sarto), **9** (Patrick Ward), **10** (Dallas and John Heaton), **11** (Michael S. Yamashita), **12** (Keren Su), **14**, **28** (Ariel Skelley), **18** (Moshe Shai), **20** (Tiziana and Gianni Baldizzone), **22** (Earl and Nazima Kowall); Getty Images p. **17**; Getty Images pp. **7** (Catherine Ledner), **15** (Uwe Krejci); Israelimages.com (Richard Nowitz) p. **19**; Mary Evans Picture Library p. **16**; Masterfile (Kevin Radford) p. **4**; Peter Sanders pp. **5**, **21**; Phil & Val Emmett p. **23**; Robert Harding p. **13**; Travel Ink (Trevor Creighton) p. **29**

Cover photograph of children at a piñata party in San Antonio, Texas, reproduced with permission of Topham Picturepoint.

The publishers would like to thank Lynne Broadbent of the BFSS National Religious Education Centre at Brunel University for her assistance in the preparation of this book.

Every effort has been made to contact copyright holders of any material reproduced in this book. Any omissions will be rectified in subsequent printings if notice is given to the publishers.

Contents

Any words printed in bold letters, **like these**,
are explained in the Glossary.

What's in a birthday?

There are lots of different kinds of birthday celebration. Most common are people's own birthdays. People may throw a big party, or just have a special meal with their family. Almost everyone gets presents and cards on their birthday, which makes them feel special.

'Happy Birthday to You'

The song many people around the world sing to wish someone happy birthday was not originally a birthday song at all. It first appeared as 'Good Morning to All', a hymn (religious song) for school children to sing at the start of the day. It only became 'Happy Birthday to You' in the 1920s or 1930s, at least 30 years after it was written!

All round the world, birthdays are celebrated with special parties and games. Often the birthday girl or boy also gets presents!

Some birthdays have special meanings. One of the most important is the birthday that celebrates the change from being a child to being adult. In most countries this happens when a person turns eighteen or twenty-one. But there are other important birthdays. For example, in Japan, the ages of three, five and seven have special meaning.

These children are celebrating the birthday of the Prophet Muhammad (pbuh).

Other birthdays are celebrated by more than one person. Often these are connected to a religion. Christians celebrate Christmas, Jesus' birthday; Muslims have the birthday of the **Prophet Muhammad (pbuh)**. Both are celebrations of the special people of the religion, so they are important to the religion's followers.

Rites of passage

In 1909, a man called Arnold van Gennep wrote about rites of passage, which mark important moments of change in a person's life. He said there are three changes in every rite of passage:

- leaving one group
- moving on to a new stage
- and joining a new group.

Kinderfeste

Many people say that Germany is the place where children's birthday parties were first held. There is even a special word for them – kinderfeste (say 'kin-der-fess-tuh'). This comes from the two words kinder (small child) and feste (party or celebration).

This girl probably doesn't know it, but today she gets presents on her birthday because of ancient kinderfeste customs!

Kinderfeste became popular in Germany about 800 years ago. In the morning of a child's birthday the candles on a cake were lit. As the candles burnt down they were replaced with new candles, so they were burning all day. Then in the evening, after dinner, the candles were blown out and the cake could finally be eaten! The blowing-out had to be done in one breath, and a wish could be made. It was said that the wish would only come true if it was secret. The birthday child was allowed to choose their favourite foods for dinner. They were also given presents.

Kinderfeste customs today

Some customs from the ancient kinderfeste still survive. Many children are given presents on their birthdays. Many still have cakes and lighted candles, and if you blow out all the candles at once you can still have a secret wish. In Germany even today, children are never given homework or chores on their birthday.

The Birthday Man

Traditionally, the Birthday Man appeared as part of a kinderfeste. He was a bearded elf who brought presents to children who had been good. Up until the early 20th century you could still buy dolls of the Birthday Man, but he has now disappeared.

This child blows out candles on their cake. Having candles on a birthday cake was part of the traditional kinderfeste celebrations.

Piñata parties

Popular in Mexico, a piñata (say 'pin-ya-ta') is a brightly decorated container, often in the shape of an animal, filled with sweets and small toys. Today most piñatas are made from papier mâché, but in the past they were made of clay pottery.

Sometimes children try to hit the piñata without wearing a blindfold. That makes it easier to hit!

Piñata song

One of the songs people sing while someone is trying to hit the piñata goes:
'I don't want nickel, I don't want silver
I only want to break the piñata!'
The words come from the days of Spanish **colonialism**. In 1557, Spanish officials toured Mexico asking people to agree to be loyal to Spain. In return, they could swap cheap nickel (a type of metal) coins for valuable silver ones.

On special occasions, such as birthdays and Christmas, a piñata is strung up so that it hangs down from the ceiling. A blindfolded person tries to break it open with a stick. People shout out directions, some of which are false to try and fool the hitter into losing their turn. If the person is successful though, the piñata breaks open and spills its contents on the ground for everyone to share.

Quinceañera

In Latin America a girl's fifteenth birthday is the day she becomes a grown-up. The celebration on this day, called a quinceañera (say 'KWIN-chay-a-NYAIR-a'), often includes a religious **ceremony** at church. Many quinceañeras include a special candle-lighting ceremony, and in some places, a young woman changes from flat shoes to high-heeled ones during the ceremony as a sign that she has grown up.

Shichi-go-san festival

When Japanese children have their third, fifth or seventh birthdays it is thought to be especially lucky. There is a special celebration on 15 November each year, called Shichi-go-san (say 'shee-chee goh san'), which means 'seven five three'. It is for children who have reached these ages during the last year.

How it began

Shichi-go-san began many centuries ago. It marked important moments in a child's life. At three, boys and girls stopped having their heads shaved and were allowed to grow their hair. At five, boys stopped wearing babyish clothes and were allowed to wear hakama (say 'ha-ka-ma'), which are like very wide-legged trousers. And at seven, girls were allowed to use an obi (say 'oh-be'), a kind of belt or sash, to tie their **kimono** (say 'kee-mo-no') instead of a cord. Shichi-go-san was one of the important rites of passage of the **Shinto** religion.

People wearing traditional Japanese clothes gather for the Shichi-go-san festival in 2002.

These two girls are wearing kimonos, ready for their Shichi-go-san celebrations.

The modern festival

Families still celebrate Shichi-go-san today. They visit Shinto **shrines** and give thanks for being healthy. Afterwards many families have a celebration meal and give their child gifts. Children still usually dress in their kimono or hakama for the ceremony, although some wear **Western**-style suits instead. The family buy special sweets called chitose-ame (meaning 'long-life sweets'). These come in bags decorated with cranes (a type of bird) and turtles, which are **symbols** of long life. The sweets are given to relatives and neighbours when the family gets home from the shrine.

Matsuo's story

Matsuo Harada, now aged 11, remembers Shichi-go-san:
'I remember my last Shichi-go-san really well. We went to the big shrine in Kagoshima, and my father rented a hakama for me to wear. There were lots of other children there too, all celebrating the festival.'

11

First birthday

In many Asian countries a child's first year is thought to be a special one. In the past many children died during their first year, and this may be why there are so many celebrations for one-year-olds.

China

When a Chinese child is one, there is a big celebration. One custom is for lots of different objects and toys to be put on the floor around the child. For example, pens, toy animals or a model car. The item that the child picks up is supposed to give a clue about what they will do when they grow up. The child that picks up a pen might become a writer; the one who picks up a car might become a racing driver.

Tigers

In China, people think that tigers protect young children. New babies are always brought gifts of clothes or toys decorated with tigers. People hope that the tigers will help save their children from illness and bad luck.

This is the kind of tiger toy that might be given to a Chinese child for luck, on their first birthday.

Chinese families celebrate the first birthday with a special meal together. In Hong Kong, for example, people eat special noodles at the birthday party. The noodles are extra-long, and are supposed to show that everyone wishes the birthday boy or girl a long life.

Korea

In Korea a child's first birthday is also special, but another celebration comes first. Paegil (say 'pay-gill') is the 100th day after a child's birth. It is a day of feasting for the child's family. Paegil dates back to the days when families celebrated the fact that their child had lived through a dangerous time and had made it to 100 days old.

A Korean child's first birthday is called tol. Family and friends all come to the party, and eat a big meal. The guests all offer the child money as a gift.

This Korean boy is celebrating tol, his first birthday, which is why he is dressed in special clothes.

Christmas

Christmas is one of the most important celebrations for **Christians**. They celebrate the day that Jesus, the key person of the Christian religion, was born. Most Christians celebrate on 25 December, but **Orthodox Christians** celebrate on 7 January.

The Bible story

The Bible (the Christian **holy** book) says that Jesus was born in a stable in a village called Bethlehem. His parents had travelled there to take part in a **census**. When they arrived there was no space in any of the inns. The only place for them to sleep was a stable, among the donkeys and sheep. Jesus was visited by three shepherds who had been told to come by an angel, and then three wise men who had followed a star from the East.

Christmas today

Today many parts of this story have found their way into our culture, even for people who are not Christians. Many people give one another presents at Christmas, even if they do not go to church. This is to remind them of the gifts of the wise men. Most **Western** houses have a Christmas tree with a star or angel on top, remembering the wise men or the shepherds.

Children in a nativity play, recreating part of the story of Jesus' birth.

Children love to open presents on Christmas Day.

Christians start to prepare for Christmas and Jesus' birthday during Advent, which begins on the Sunday nearest to 30 November. Christmas ends on **Epiphany**, 6 January, 12 days after Christmas Day, when families take down their Christmas decorations.

Many Christians go to church on Christmas Eve (24 December) as they remember Jesus' birthday. There are also church services on Christmas Day, and people gather with their families and give each other presents.

Pierre's story

Pierre Villefranche, aged 14, describes Christmas in Belgium:

'We give small family presents at Christmas. We put them under the tree or in stockings at night, to be found on Christmas Day. Christmas breakfast is cougnou, a kind of sweet bread in a shape that's meant to be like baby Jesus.'

Christmas customs

People celebrate Christmas in lots of different ways. Many remind us of the Bible story of the birth of Jesus – the angel or star on a Christmas tree, for example. Others have their beginnings in birthday celebrations around the world.

Giving presents

Giving presents is a common way of celebrating a birthday. Almost two centuries ago, in the 1800s, Saint Nicholas became a popular **symbol** of gift-giving in many European countries. He brought presents to children on the eve of his feast day. Saint Nicholas is now often called Father Christmas or Santa Claus.

The first Christmas card was created by the Englishman John Calcott Horsley in 1843. It looked like a postcard and showed a large family enjoying a Christmas celebration. The message read, 'A Merry Christmas and a Happy New Year to You'. About 1000 of the cards were sold.

Decorations

People all round the world decorate their homes for birthday celebrations. At Christmas many people have Christmas trees. These were probably first used in Germany in the early 1600s. Before this, people had decorated a 'Paradise Tree' as part of a popular play staged all over Germany on Christmas Eve. Eventually the custom of decorating a tree spread around the world.

Decorations hang from a Christmas tree. The first Christmas trees had wafers hanging from them. The wafers stood for the body of Jesus Christ, whose birthday is celebrated at Christmas.

La Befana

In Italy, the kindly, wrinkled old woman La Befana (say 'Lah Bef-ah-nah') brings presents on the eve of 5 January, the day before **Epiphany**. According to legend, the wise men asked her to come with them to see the infant Jesus. She refused, saying she was too busy and had to clean her house, and so she missed the wondrous sight. Each year, La Befana goes from house to house, leaving gifts and looking for the Christ child.

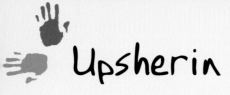

Upsherin

Upsherin (say 'upp-share-inn') is a haircut, but a very important one. In some Jewish families boys do not have their hair cut until they are three years old. Then it is cut in a special **ceremony**. Often friends and family are there – traditionally it is they who take the first snips. Often long strands called peyos (say 'pay-ohs') are left just above the ears. These are worn because of a passage in the Torah (the Jewish **holy** book) that says hair should not be cut too short on the sides of the head.

Why wait three years?

A passage in the Torah says that the fruit of a tree should not be cut off and eaten for its first three years. Some **Jews** think that this means children's hair should also not be cut for the first three years of their lives.

This little boy has just had the first snips of hair taken off as part of his upsherin haircut

What is special about upsherin?

Upsherin marks the moment when a baby becomes a child. After upsherin a boy is allowed to wear special items of clothing worn by adult men, such as a yarmulke (say 'yar-mool-kuh'), which is a small cap worn on the top of the head. He also begins his religious training after upsherin.

Bar and bat mitzvah

Bar mitzvah is a Jewish celebration for boys and bat mitzvah is a celebration for girls. They mark the move from being a child to having the same duties as an adult. They happen when boys are thirteen and girls are twelve. The ceremonies involve the boy or girl reading the Torah in public in Hebrew, to show that they are taking on an adult position.

This girl is reading from the Torah. This is a very important part of her bat mitzvah celebration.

The Birthday of the Prophet

The Birthday of the Prophet is an important celebration. It is held on the birthday of the **Prophet Muhammad (pbuh)**, the key person of the **Muslim** religion. Not all Muslims celebrate it, however. In some countries, for example Saudi Arabia, the day passes by much like any other.

Where the Birthday of the Prophet is celebrated, for example in Egypt and Turkey, it is a happy time. Families come together to have a celebration meal. People spend money they have saved up on sweets, toys, clothes and other treats.

These Muslims in Niger have gathered together to celebrate the Birthday of the Prophet.

This one-week-old Muslim baby is having its head shaved very carefully!

People tell stories of the Prophet Muhammad (pbuh), read poetry and sing songs to praise him. There are also readings from the Qur'an (say 'kor-ARN') and some families give food and money to the poor.

Many families visit a mosque (Muslim place of worship) to hear the priest speaking about the Prophet Muhammad (pbuh). Those outside the mosque do not miss out. Loudspeakers mean that everyone can hear.

Silver-haired babies

Many wealthy Muslims give thanks after a child is born by giving gifts to the poor. After the child is a week old, its head is shaved. Its family then gives an amount of silver equal to the weight of the child's hair. Often extra silver is given too. After this, family and friends meet for a feast where the child is named. Some of the food from the feast is also given to poor people.

Gurpurb

The **Sikh** religion is based on the teachings of ten great men, its first leaders. These leaders were called gurus, and their birthdays are among the most important events of the year for Sikhs. The celebration of a guru's birthday is called a gurpurb (say 'gurr-purr-buh').

Guru Nanak's Birthday

Guru Nanak was the first guru of Sikhism. His gurpurb celebrations usually happen in the month of November. They begin two days before the actual birthday, with a non-stop reading of the Siri Guru Granth Sahib (say 'goo-roo gran-th saa-hib'), the Sikh **holy** book. One day before the birthday, a great procession is organized including religious leaders and ordinary worshippers.

These Sikh girls are wearing traditional dress at the gurpurb for Guru Nanak in New Delhi, India.

Guru Nanak's birthday itself begins at 4 or 5 a.m., when the reading of the Siri Guru Granth Sahib has finished. There are special religious songs, readings from the Siri Guru Granth Sahib and talks about the meaning of the Guru's words. This goes on until about 2 p.m. Then people are given a sweet pudding called karah parshad, followed by a meal. This is always eaten at the end of a service at the gurdwara. There can also be a night-time celebration, which ends at about 2 a.m. By that time, many people have been awake for about 22 hours!

Guru Nanak, founder of the Sikh religion, whose birthday (gurpurb) is celebrated each year by Sikhs everywhere.

Tegh's story

Tegh Singh, aged 11, from Lahore in India describes a gurpurb:

'*The gurpurb for Guru Nanak Sahib is a great celebration for Sikhs here in Lahore. The Guru was born very near to here, so we feel especially proud. People come from all over the world to visit the birthplace, and the procession through the streets of Lahore is a great colourful, noisy event.*'

Rama Navami

One of the great **Hindu** birthday celebrations is a nine-day festival called Rama Navami (say 'rama nah-va-mee'), in March or April. It leads up to the birthday of Rama, the human form of the Hindu god Vishnu. Rama's story is told in a long poem called the Ramayana. In it, Rama's beautiful wife Sita is kidnapped by a demon king called Ravana. Rama follows and, after many adventures, kills the demon king with an arrow and saves Sita.

Hindu birthday traditions

On a Hindu child's first birthday, his or her head is shaved. Removal of the hair cleanses the child of any evil in past lives, **symbolizing** a renewal of the soul. Hindu children only celebrate their birthdays until they are sixteen.

This Hindu boy is having his head shaved on his first birthday.

Celebrations

Rama Navami is especially important in the northern Indian city of Ayodhya, where Rama was born. A huge fair is organized for two days. Chariot processions leave from the temples, taking statues of Rama and Sita on tours through the city. The processions include people dressed in scenes from the Ramayana. Some people fast (go without food) on the actual day of Rama's birthday.

A Rama Navami celebration of the birthday of the man-god Rama, in India. In the background picture are Rama, Sita, Hanuman and Lakshman, characters from the Ramayana.

Meera's story

Meera Shastri, aged 9, remembers Rama Navami in Jammu, India in 2001:

'This year the whole City of Temples was decorated with flags. The Maharani (wife of an Indian prince or ruler) came to visit the poor people and handed out 80 blankets and 10 sewing machines. My mother got one of the sewing machines!'

Wesak

Wesak is the festival of Buddha's birthday. **Buddhists** believe that Buddha was a man who achieved what they call 'enlightenment'. This meant that he had reached the highest state of spiritual or religious understanding possible, and was free from the cares of the world.

There are two main types of Buddhism. The first type is found in south-east Asia (Thailand, Myanmar, Laos, for example). Its followers celebrate the birth, enlightenment and death of Buddha all on the same day. This is on the first full moon in May (except in a leap year, when the festival is held in June). The second type of Buddhism is followed in central and east Asia (China, Japan, Tibet).

These Wesak celebrations are happening at a Buddhist temple in Wimbledon, London.

Wesak celebrations may include visiting the temple to think about Buddha. Most Buddhists will decorate their houses with pandals, Wesak lanterns and oil lamps. Pandals are made of bamboo canes covered in coloured paper or cloth. Some Buddhists may send Wesak cards to friends during the month of May.

Many lanterns have been used to decorate this house for Wesak celebrations.

Catherine's story

Catherine Ngo, now aged 15, describes Wesak celebrations in Vietnam:

'I remember the Wesak celebrations from before we moved here to America, back in Vietnam. There are many Buddhists there, so lots of people celebrate the Buddha's birthday. People would decorate their houses with lanterns and garlands (strings of flowers). Some people set free caged birds, which stands for the **compassion** of the Buddha.'

27

National birthdays

In 1909 Arnold van Gennep said that a rite of passage involves three rules: leaving a group, moving on to a new stage, and joining a new group. Although he was talking about individuals, his rules can be applied to groups of people, even whole countries. When a country becomes independent it goes through a rite of passage. For example, in 1946 India was part of the group of countries that made up the **British Empire**. Then, on 15 August 1947, it moved on to a new stage and became an independent country. It joined a new group – the group of countries that make their own decisions and deal with their own problems.

The day on which a country becomes independent can be thought of as its birthday. People often have parties and celebrations on this day. One of the biggest and most famous is 4 July in the USA. This is the anniversary of the day when they became independent – 4 July 1776.

These girls have dressed in patriotic costume to enjoy Independence Day in the USA, 2001.

These celebrations in Sydney Harbour were for Australia Day, 1998.

Today, many of the world's cities have large fireworks displays on their country's national birthdays. There are parades, games, concerts, speeches and picnics. Some of the world's biggest national birthday celebrations happen in Australia (Australia Day, 26 January), on Bastille Day (France, 14 July) and Independence Day in Mexico (16 September).

Year of Independence

The best-ever year for Independence Days was 1960. Eighteen countries became independent: Somalia, Cyprus, Nigeria, Benin, Burkina Faso, Cameroon, the Central African Republic, Chad, Congo, Côte d'Ivoire, Gabon, Madagascar, Mali, Mauritania, Niger, Senegal, Togo and Zaire.

Glossary

British Empire parts of the world that were ruled by Britain, mainly during the 19th and the first half of the 20th centuries. It covered much of the world, including large parts of the Caribbean, Africa and the Indian subcontinent.

Buddhists (Buddhism) people who follow the way of life taught by the Buddha, who lived in ancient India about 2500 years ago. The Buddha was not a god, but a man. He taught his followers how to live simple, peaceful lives.

census survey taken to count the number of people living in a specific area, as well as the jobs they do, their ages and other details about their lives

ceremony a special ritual or celebration

Christians (Christianity) people who follow the religion of Christianity, which is based on the teachings of Jesus Christ. Christians believe that Jesus was the Son of God.

colonialism process of taking over and ruling another country, making it a colony. For example, when Britain ruled India, India was a British colony.

compassion pity, especially the type of pity that leads people to be helpful or kind to others

Epiphany day of the appearance of the wise men to visit the new born baby Jesus, which Christians celebrate on 6 January

Hindus (Hinduism) people who follow Hinduism. Hindus worship one god (called Brahman) in many forms. Hinduism is the main religion in India.

holy special because it is to do with God or a religious purpose

Jews (Judaism) people who follow the religion of Judaism. Jews pray to one god. Their holy book is the Hebrew Bible, sometimes called the Old Testament by Christians.

kimono traditional Japanese robe, often made of silk

Muslims (Islam) people who follow the religion of Islam. Muslims pray to one God, whom they call Allah.

Orthodox Christians members of a branch of Christianity that developed separately from the Roman Catholic Church. Roman Catholicism grew up in the West, Orthodox Christianity in the East.

Prophet Muhammad (pbuh) the key person of the Muslim religion. When his name is written, peace and blessings be upon him (pbuh) always appears after it.

Shinto ancient Japanese religion in which nature is very important

shrine place of worship that is linked with someone who has died, for example a saint

Sikhs (Sikhism) people who follow the religion of Sikhism, based on the teachings of the ten Gurus, or teachers

symbol/symbolize when a picture, object or action stands for something else

Western something from Europe, North America and Australasia or from that culture

Further resources

More books to read

Births, Jacqueline Dineen (Hodder Children's Books, 2000)

Celebrations (series), Anita Ganeri (Heinemann Library, 2001)

Guru Nanak's Birthday, Margaret Davidson (Religious and Moral Education Press)

Horrible Christmas, Terry Deary (Scholastic Hippo, 2000)

Religions of the World (series), Sue Penney (Heinemann Library, 2002)

Index

Celel

Divali

Anita Ganeri

Heinemann
LIBRARY

www.heinemann.co.uk/library
Visit our website to find out more information about Heinemann Library books.

To order:
☎ Phone 44 (0) 1865 888066
▤ Send a fax to 44 (0) 1865 314091
▢ Visit the Heinemann Bookshop at www.heinemann.co.uk/library to browse our catalogue and order online.

First published in Great Britain by Heinemann Library,
Halley Court, Jordan Hill, Oxford OX2 8EJ
a division of Reed Educational and Professional Publishing Ltd.
Heinemann is a registered trademark of Reed Educational & Professional Publishing Ltd.

OXFORD MELBOURNE AUCKLAND
JOHANNESBURG BLANTYRE GABORONE
IBADAN PORTSMOUTH (NH) USA CHICAGO

© Reed Educational and Professional Publishing Ltd 2002
The moral right of the proprietor has been asserted.

Designed by Celia Floyd
Originated by Ambassador Litho Ltd
Printed by Wing King Tong in Hong Kong

ISBN 0 431 13793 5 (hardback)   ISBN 0 431 13801 X (paperback)
06 05 04 03 02   06 05 04 03 02
10 9 8 7 6 5 4 3 2   10 9 8 7 6 5 4 3 2 1

British Library Cataloguing in Publication Data

Ganeri, Anita
    Divali. – (Celebrations)
    1. Divali – Juvenile literature
    I. Title
    394.2'6545

Acknowledgements
The Publishers would like to thank the following for permission to reproduce photographs:
Andes Press Agency: Carlos Reyes-Manzo p14; Ann and Bury Peerless: pp6, 7; Christine Osborne Pictures: p12: Corbis: Tim Hawkins (Eye Ubiquitous) p4, Arvind Garg p8; Dinodia Picture Agency: p19, 20, Sudheer Babji p15; ffotograff: Patricia Aithie p18; Hutchison Library: Liba Taylor p5, Michael Macintyre p21; Judy Harrison/Format: p9; Sally Greenhill: p11: Sarah Thorley: p10; Trip: H Rogers pp13, 16, 17

Cover photograph reproduced with permission of Trip: A Tovy

Our thanks to the Bradford Interfaith Education Centre for their comments in the preparation of this book.

Every effort has been made to contact copyright holders of any material reproduced in this book. Any omissions will be rectified in subsequent printings if notice is given to the Publisher.

Contents

Words printed in **bold letters like these** are explained in the glossary.

Festival of lights

In October or November, **Hindus** celebrate the festival of Divali. This is a very happy time in the Hindu year. Divali is the Hindu festival of light. People decorate their homes with small lights, called **divas**. Strings of twinkling fairylights light up the streets. People send each other Divali cards and give gifts of sweets and new clothes.

A street decorated for Divali. The decoration shows that the name of the festival can be spelt differently.

Children lighting diva lamps for Divali.

There are many reasons for celebrating Divali. Some people remember the story of Prince Rama. Long ago, he defeated the evil demon, Ravana, and came home to be crowned king. People also **worship Lakshmi**, the goddess of wealth and good fortune. For some Hindus, Divali is the start of the new year. Wherever Divali is celebrated, its message is the same. It is a time for celebrating the triumph of good over evil and of hope for a happy future.

The story of Rama and Sita

At Divali, **Hindus** remember the story of Prince Rama. Long ago, King Dasaratha ruled a **kingdom** in north India. Prince Rama was his eldest son and the **heir** to his throne. But Rama's stepmother wanted her son, Prince Bharata, to be king instead. Rama was sent to live in the forest. He could not return home for many years. His wife, Sita, and his brother, Lakshman, went with him.

Rama, Sita and Lakshman in the forest.

One day, Rama and Lakshman were out hunting. While they were gone, a **holy** man came to Sita's door and begged her for food. But the holy man was really Ravana, an evil demon king, in disguise. He kidnapped Sita and carried her off to his palace in Lanka. He wanted to marry Sita but Sita refused.

Prince Rama

Rama is one of the most popular Hindu gods. Hindus believe that he is the god **Vishnu** in a different form. Vishnu came to Earth several times to save the world from danger. This time he came as a royal prince. Hindus **worship** Rama as a hero. He was brave and wise, and loved Sita very much.

Rama and Sita (centre and right) and Lakshman (left).

Rama to the rescue

Hanuman, the monkey general, who helped Rama to rescue Sita.

Rama and Lakshman searched for Sita in the forest. But they could not find her. Then a bird told Rama where Sita was. Hanuman, the monkey general, offered to help Rama. He gathered a huge army together, and set off to the palace in Lanka to rescue Sita. Ravana was furious. He sent his own army of giants and demons to fight them off. A terrible battle raged.

Finally, Rama met Ravana in battle. He killed Ravana with a golden bow and arrow, given to him by the gods. Then he and Sita were reunited. By now, fourteen years had passed and Rama and Sita could go home. People lit lamps to show them the way and to show how good had won over evil. Today, at Divali, **Hindus** still light lamps to welcome Rama and Sita home.

The *Ramayana*

The story of Rama and Sita is told in a long poem called the *Ramayana*. It is one of the Hindus' **holy** books. Hindu children can read the story in comic books and watch it on video or on television.

Children acting out the story of Rama and Sita.

Divali celebrations

Hindus celebrating Divali in the mandir.

In India, Divali lasts for up to five days. It is holiday time for everyone. In Britain, **Hindus** celebrate Divali on the nearest weekend. Many Hindus visit the **mandir** to celebrate with their families and friends. They make offerings of food and flowers to the **deities**. They believe that this is a way of showing and **worshipping** God. In return, they receive God's blessing. This is called **puja**. There is a special puja at Divali weekend.

Divali is also a time for having fun. After the puja, there is music and dancing. The stick dance is very popular. Each dancer has a pair of sticks. They dance around each other, tapping each other's sticks in time to the music. The faster the music, the faster you bang your sticks. You have to mind your fingers! In another dance, dancers hold a **diva** in their hands. But the day is not over yet. There is still the grand firework display to come.

Stick dancing at Divali.

Good fortune

Divali is also the time when **Hindus** remember the goddess **Lakshmi**. She is **Vishnu**'s wife and the goddess of wealth and good fortune. People light **divas** to welcome Lakshmi into their homes. They hope that she will bring them good luck in the year to come. Some people clean their homes from top to bottom, ready for Lakshmi to bless them.

Lakshmi, the goddess of wealth and good luck.

Divali is an important time for Hindu business people. This is when they close their old **account book** and open a new one. They bring their account books to the **mandir** and place a pile of coins on top. Then they perform a special **puja** to Lakshmi. They ask her to bring them good fortune in the new year.

An accounting ceremony at Divali.

Divali cards

Many Hindus send Divali cards to each other. Try making your own. Decorate it with a picture of Lakshmi or some divas. Write 'Happy Divali' inside the card.

Lights and patterns

Divali gets its name from the word *Deepavali* which means 'rows of lights'. Traditionally, people light small clay lamps, filled with oil. These lamps are called **divas**. In Britain, some people put strings of fairy lights around their windows. Lights are also put up in some streets. The lights are for welcoming **Lakshmi** and celebrating Rama and Sita coming home. They also show how good always drives evil away, just as the light drives away darkness.

Diva lights and Divali food.

At Divali, people draw colourful patterns on the doorsteps of their houses. This is to welcome in Lakshmi. These patterns are called rangoli. People use coloured chalk, sand, flour and rice. A favourite pattern for Divali is the **lotus flower** because it is a sign of Lakshmi. In Britain, some **mandirs** hold a rangoli competition for children. The best design wins a prize.

A rangoli pattern.

Divali patterns

Draw your own rangoli pattern with a flower shape in the centre. Use coloured paper and paints. Decorate it with a sprinkle of glitter, coloured sand, rice or lentils.

Food and clothes

Divali is a festival for sharing with family and friends. Many **Hindus** give each other presents. Sometimes this is a piece of silver or gold jewellery. Sometimes it is a set of new clothes. This is a reminder that Divali brings a new year and a time of new beginnings.

At Divali, Hindus eat special food. They may have a Divali meal at home or in the **mandir**. People give boxes of sweets to their friends and relatives. Indian sweets are made of milk products, coconut, nuts and sugar. They are very sweet indeed! People make sweets at home or buy them from sweet-shops.

Indian sweets for Divali.

A girl dressed in her new Divali clothes.

The last day of Divali is called Bhaiya Dooj. It is a time for brothers to visit their sisters' homes. Here they are treated to a delicious meal. In return, the brother promises to look after his sister. He gives her some money, jewellery or clothes as a sign of his love and support. A story explains how this custom began. Long ago, Yama, the angel of death, visited his sister on this day and ate a special meal. He ordered everyone to do the same.

Sikh Divali

Divali is also an important festival for **Sikhs**. This is the time when they remember one of their great teachers, **Guru** Hargobind. He lived in India about 400 years ago. The **emperor** put Guru Hargobind in prison, together with 52 **Hindu** princes. The time came for the Guru to be set free. But he would leave only if all the Hindu princes were allowed to go with him. The emperor agreed.

A Sikh woman lighting a diva.

At Divali, Sikhs celebrate Guru Hargobind's release from prison. They light candles and lamps to welcome the Guru home. Many Sikhs visit the **gurdwara** to **worship**. They remember how Guru Hargobind showed Sikhs that when all peaceful efforts fail, they need to fight to protect what they believe in. Afterwards, they share a meal. The day ends with a firework display.

In India, Harimandir Sahib (the Golden Temple) in Amritsar is lit up with rows of twinkling lights. People float candles in the lake around the temple. It is a very important **shrine** for Sikhs. Amritsar was Guru Hargobind's home.

The Golden Temple at Amritsar.

Around the world

Hindus all over the world celebrate Divali. Most Hindus live in India. There, Divali celebrations can last for five whole days. On the first evening, people light a single lamp for Yama, the angel of death. An image of **Lakshmi** is washed in milk. On the second day, people get up early and eat a special breakfast. They remember the story of how **Krishna** killed a terrible demon called Narakasur and released the princesses he had captured. The third day of Divali is for worshipping Lakshmi. It is also the end of the old year.

Divali fireworks in Bombay, India.

The fourth day of Divali is a time for new starts. It is a day filled with hope for the future. People give gifts of new clothes and jewellery. They remember the story of Rama and how he rescued Sita from wicked Ravana. **Divas** are lit and there are lots of fireworks. In Britain, Hindus also remember these stories in their celebrations.

The last day is Brother's Day. This is when brothers visit their sisters to enjoy a sumptuous feast. Then Divali is over, for another year.

Indonesian shadow puppets are used to tell the story of Rama and Sita.

Hindu festival calendar

January/February	Vasant Panchami/Saraswati Puja (A festival marking the coming of spring and for remembering Saraswati, goddess of art and learning)
February/March	Mahashivratri (A festival for the god Shiva)
February/March	Holi (A festival for remembering Krishna's life and for celebrating spring)
March/April	Ramnavami (Rama's birthday)
March/April	Hanuman Jayanti (Hanuman's birthday)
August	Raksha Bandhan (Sister's and Brother's Day)
August/September	Janmashtami (Krishna's birthday)
August/September	Ganesha Chaturthi (Ganesha's birthday)
September/October	Dassehra/Ma-Durga Puja/ Navaratri (Remembers Rama and Sita, and Ma-Durga)
October/November	Divali (The festival of light)

Glossary

account book book in which business people keep a record of the money they have earned or spent

deity god or goddess. Hindus believe in a great spirit called Brahman or God. They also worship many deities. Each deity shows a different part of God's power. Avatar is another word for God.

diva small clay lamp that is lit at Divali

emperor powerful ruler

gurdwara place where Sikhs worship

Guru one of ten great Sikh spiritual teachers

heir when a king dies, the heir is the person who becomes the next king

Hindu person who follows the Hindu religion, which began in India thousands of years ago

holy to do with God or a religious teacher

kingdom country that is ruled over by a king

Krishna name of a popular Hindu god

Lakshmi the goddess of wealth and good fortune

lotus flower flower that grows in ponds and rivers. It is a special flower for Hindus.

mandir place where Hindus worship. It is sometimes called a temple.

puja how Hindus worship. They offer flowers and sweets to the deities and receive God's blessing.

shrine holy place where deities are worshipped

Sikh person who follows the Sikh religion, which began in India about 500 years ago

Vishnu name of a great Hindu god. He protects the world from harm.

worship to show respect and love to God

Index